SRA

Reading Mastery®

Transformations

Reading
Textbook A

Siegfried Engelmann

Owen Engelmann

Karen Davis

McGraw
Hill

Acknowledgments

The authors are grateful to the following people for their assistance in the preparations of Reading Mastery Transformations Grade 1 Reading.

Joanna Jachowicz
Blake Engelmann
Charlene Tolles-Engelmann
Cally Dwyer
Melissa Morrow
Toni Reeves

Emily Jachowicz for her valuable student input

We'd also like to acknowledge, from McGraw Hill, the valuable contributions by:

Mary Eisele
Nancy Stigers
Jason Yanok

mheducation.com/prek-12

Send all inquiries to:
McGraw-Hill Education
8787 Orion Place
Columbus, OH 43240

ISBN: 978-0-07-905405-0
MHID: 0-07-905405-6

Printed in the United States of America.

1 2 3 4 5 6 7 8 9 LWI 24 23 22 21 20

1. kept
2. yes
3. get
4. getting
5. then

1. dream
2. liked
3. named
4. over
5. thing
6. sing

1. tired
2. same
3. row
4. time
5. late
6. here

Bob and Jan
Part One

Jan liked to do the same thing over and over.

One time, she made a shirt that she liked. So she made the same shirt over and over.

One time, she made rock turtles over and over.

Jan had a pal named Bob. She told Bob to come over to her home and sing with her. Bob asked his dad, "Can I go over to Jan's home?"

Bob's dad said, "Yes, but you must come home by nine. Don't be late."

When Bob got to Jan's home, she told him, "First I will sing. Then you will sing."

Jan started to sing, "Row, row, row your boat . . ." But she did not sing it just one time. She did the same thing over and over and over.

More next time.

1. getting
2. bet
3. better
4. kept
5. sell
6. when

1. only
2. singing
3. tub
4. duck
5. thing
6. cow

1. taste
2. tired
3. year
4. shine
5. boat
6. while

1. wig
2. which
3. such
4. sixth
5. stop
6. sand

5

Bob and Jan
Part Two

Jan kept singing the same thing over and over. It was getting late. And Bob was getting tired. But Jan just kept singing, "Row, row, row your boat . . ." over and over.

At last, Jan's mom said to Jan, "Don't you think it is time for Bob to have a turn singing?"

"Yes," Jan said. So Bob had a turn. "You are my sunshine . . ."

When he was done, Jan said, "I like the way you sing. Do it one more time." So Bob did it one more time.

When Bob was done, Jan said the same thing she said before. And Bob did the same thing he did before.

At last, Jan's mom said, "Don't you think it is time for Bob to go home?"

Do you think Bob got home on time? No. He was late. He ran, but he was not home by nine.

Bob will not be singing with Jan for a while.

The end.

1. tasted
2. hope
3. sale
4. y<u>ea</u>r
5. l<u>oa</u>ded
6. cak<u>e</u>s

1. thank
2. think
3. drink
4. sank

1. last
2. sell
3. turtle
4. h<u>er</u>
5. pots
6. pans

1. <u>bitter</u>
2. <u>butter</u>
3. <u>better</u>
4. <u>batter</u>
5. li<u>tt</u>le
6. <u>hotter</u>

1. hat
2. hop
3. set
4. such

Better Batter
Part One

Last year, a fox sold bitter butter to a little turtle. That turtle's mom made cake batter with that bitter butter. The cake was bad, bad, bad.

So the little turtle and her mom made a cake for the fox and told him to eat it. He did. That cake was so bitter that he had to dive into the pond and drink, drink, drink.

10

Then the fox <u>told</u> the little turtle and h<u>er</u> mom, "That is the last time I will sell bitter butter."

This y<u>ea</u>r, the fox made a big tub <u>of</u> butter. He said, "I made a lot <u>of</u> butter. I hope it is not bitter butter."

He tasted a little bit of his butter. Then he jumped up and down and said, "This is better than other butter. It is so sweet and fine."

More next time.

1. thank
2. thing
3. sing
4. sang
5. wing
6. hang

1. some
2. come
3. done
4. none
5. one

1. they
2. there
3. here
4. were

1. easy
2. yell
3. filled
4. rolls
5. sale
6. fear

1. sells
2. turned
3. sixth
4. flying

Better Batter
Part Two

The fox had made a big tub of butter. Was that butter bitter? No. It was sweet. The fox said, "It will be easy to sell this better butter."

So he filled pots and pans with his butter. He loaded them into his cart. Then he started down the road with his pots and pans. "I have sweet butter for sale," he said.

14

Five birds were near that road. The fox said, "Do you like sweet butter?"

One bird said, "We know the taste of your butter, and it is not sweet. You sold us some last year. It was bitter."

"But this butter is better," the fox said. "Come over here and taste some."

"No thanks," the birds said. "We don't like the taste of your butter."

So the fox hiked down the road with his pots and pans. At last, he came to a rat. He told the rat that he had sweet butter.

The rat said, "I can eat a lot of bad things, but not your butter. It is too bitter for me."

More to come.

1. wore
2. r<u>oll</u>
3. know
4. throw

1. w<u>e</u>r<u>e</u>
2. <u>t</u>urned
3. summer
4. first
5. tast<u>e</u>r
6. h<u>ur</u>ts

1. yello<u>w</u>
2. they
3. them
4. best
5. red
6. set

1. dress
2. sixth
3. there
4. rid
5. pigs
6. ducks

1. wig
2. stop
3. sand
4. such
5. whi<u>ch</u>

Better Batter
Part Three

The fox had sweet butter to sell. Did the birds taste it? Did the rat taste it?

At last, the fox came to some goats. "Sweet, sweet butter for sale," he said.

One goat said, "Last year, I made rolls with some of your butter. Those rolls were so bitter that I had to throw them away."

The fox said, "But this butter is better. Come over and taste some."

The goats just turned away.

The fox hiked down the road to the barn. The fox asked the ducks to taste his butter. Then he asked the pigs, rams, and cows the same thing.

But they just told him, "Go home with your bitter butter."

This cake is fine.

The fox was sad. He did not know <u>what</u> to do. So he sat down and started to think. Then he said, "I know. I will make a cake for the summer Cake Bake."

And that is <u>what</u> he did.

He first made cake batter. He said, "This batter has better butter. Batter with better butter won't be bitter."

He baked a big yellow cake with his batter, and it was fine.

More to come.

1. only
2. tasters
3. hurry
4. began
5. flying
6. summer

1. each
2. reach
3. birds
4. red
5. rid
6. wig

1. dress
2. white
3. spring
4. brothers
5. sisters
6. best

1. days
2. weeks
3. returned
4. planned
5. yellow

Better Batter
Part Four

The fox said, "No one will eat this cake if they know that I made it." So the fox wore a red wig, a dress, and a big hat. He said, "Now they will not know me."

There were 20 cakes in the Cake Bake. Six cake tasters said, "We will eat a little bit of each cake and see which cake is best."

They ate a little bit of the other cakes. But when they came to the big yellow cake, they ate a lot.

One cake taster said, "I can't stop eating this cake. It is so fine."

Four other cake tasters said, "This is the best cake we have tasted."

The sixth cake taster asked, "Why did I get only a little bit of this cake?"

Just then, the fox got rid of his hat, his wig, and his dress. He told the cake tasters, "That is my cake. The batter is made with my better butter."

Now the fox makes a lot of sweet butter, and he sells it fast. Birds, pigs, rats, cows, and turtles s<u>a</u>y that it is the best butter they have tasted.

The end.

7

1. sing
2. wing
3. sang
4. hang
5. rang

1. summer
2. sister
3. brother
4. winter
5. hotter
6. Vern

1. pants
2. hurry
3. still
4. stayed
5. short
6. sunburn

1. sky
2. Tom
3. Irma
4. shade
5. went
6. set

I have a f<u>ea</u>r of flying.

Can Tom Fly?

It was spring. The other birds were set to fly, but Tom was not set to fly.

Tom had a f<u>ea</u>r of flying. He told his mom, "I can run, and I can r<u>ea</u>d. I can sit, and I can sing. But I do not think I can fly."

Each day, Tom's brothers and sisters went flying, but Tom stayed at home.

Each day, the others came home and told what fun they had. Tom did not have fun.

Then just before summer started, Tom's mom told him, "It's time for you to fly. Jump up on my back and hang on."

He did that. And his mom s<u>ai</u>led into the sky.

Then Tom's mother said, "It is more fun if you hold your wings up."

After he did that, was he still on his mom's back? No. He was not on his mom's back. He was flying. And it was fun.

The end.

8

1. t<u>ur</u>n
2. b<u>ur</u>n
3. thank
4. sank
5. snow
6. slow

1. <u>wai</u>ting
2. <u>be</u>gan
3. <u>sandy</u>
4. <u>wi</u>nter
5. r<u>ea</u>ch

1. five
2. ride
3. white
4. bike
5. shade
6. wore

1. <u>bur</u>ned
2. <u>planned</u>
3. sun<u>burned</u>
4. sh<u>or</u>t
5. h<u>a</u>rd
6. <u>pants</u>

Vern and His Burn
Part One

The winter was h<u>a</u>rd and cold. <u>I</u>rma and h<u>er</u> brother V<u>er</u>n were w<u>ai</u>ting for spring. <u>I</u>rma said, "We have not seen the sun for weeks. We have only seen a d<u>a</u>rk sky."

At last spring came, but things were still cold.

It feels like summer.

After five days of rain, the sun began to shine. The day turned hotter and hotter. Vern said to his sister, "It feels like summer."

Irma said, "I think I'm going to ride my bike to the lake and see the birds."

Vern planned to ride with her. Irma wore a
big hat. Vern did not have a hat. He did not have a
shirt. The only thing he wore was short pants.

More to come.

9

1. your
2. you're
3. shark
4. swim
5. swam
6. hunt

1. thinking
2. sinking
3. closer
4. bigger
5. sandy
6. really

1. beat
2. bet
3. not
4. note
5. rain
6. ran

1. hop
2. beach
3. shade
4. shore
5. how
6. pink

33

Vern and His Burn
Part Two

Irma and Vern were on the way to the lake. The sun was hot. Irma told her brother, "You are as white as snow. I think the sun may be too hot for you."

"No way," Vern said.

Irma said, "But I know the sun will burn you if you don't have your shirt on."

"Not me," Vern said. "I don't get sunburned."

After <u>I</u>rma and h<u>er</u> brother rod<u>e</u> to the lak<u>e</u>, V<u>er</u>n stopped at a shor<u>e</u> that had a sandy beach. He told his sister, "I think I will st<u>ay</u> on this beach so the sun can make me r<u>ea</u>lly hot."

<u>I</u>rma said, "I am going to the other sid<u>e</u> of the lak<u>e</u> and see the birds. I hop<u>e</u> you st<u>ay</u> in the shad<u>e</u>."

"I will have fun in the sun," V<u>er</u>n said. "I will see you lat<u>er</u>."

More to come.

1. when
2. then
3. where
4. there
5. pink
6. sink

1. red
2. next
3. well
4. shell
5. st<u>a</u>yed
6. became

1. one
2. once
3. does
4. doesn't
5. wasn't
6. you're

1. re<u>tur</u>n
2. <u>a</u>rms
3. h<u>ur</u>t
4. <u>j</u>umper
5. <u>sl</u>ip
6. st<u>and</u>

Vern and His Burn
Part Three

When Irma was over on the f<u>ar</u> side of the lake, the sun got hotter and hotter. Vern did not r<u>oll</u> over. He just st<u>ay</u>ed on the sand. At first, he became a little pink. After a while, he started to get re<u>a</u>lly pink.

At last his sister ret<u>ur</u>ned. She asked him, "How do you feel, Vern?"

"I feel fine," he told her. "That sun is not t<u>oo</u> hot for me."

Later that day, Vern said other things like, "Ow, that h<u>ur</u>ts. Ow, my back h<u>ur</u>ts."

By the time Vern and Irma were home, Vern was not pink. He was red.

Vern's mom said, "You have a bad sunburn. Why didn't you take a shirt and a hat with you?"

Vern said, "I didn't think I'd get sunburned, but I will know better next time."

The end.

1. there
2. they
3. well
4. best
5. yes
6. yell

1. believe
2. G<u>or</u>man
3. listen
4. wasn't
5. jumper
6. once

1. sail
2. goat
3. play
4. say
5. toad
6. h<u>ar</u>d

1. pal
2. p<u>ai</u>l
3. liked
4. hiked
5. sink
6. r<u>oll</u>

The Goat and the Pail

A goat named Gorman did not see well. He liked to play with his pals, but his pals did not like to play with him. They said, "It is no fun to play with a goat that runs into you time after time."

One day, the pals were playing with a pail. One pal was a toad who liked to hop over the pail. The fox liked to jump over the pail, too. The pig didn't jump over the pail. She ate the corn that was in the pail.

Gorman told the other pals, "I can jump over that pail."

The pals said, "We do not think you can."

One pal said, "You say you can jump over it, but you will just run into it."

"No," Gorman said. "I may be the best pail jumper there is." So Gorman jumped.

Did he run into the pail? No.

Did he jump over the pail? No.

What did he do? You will see.

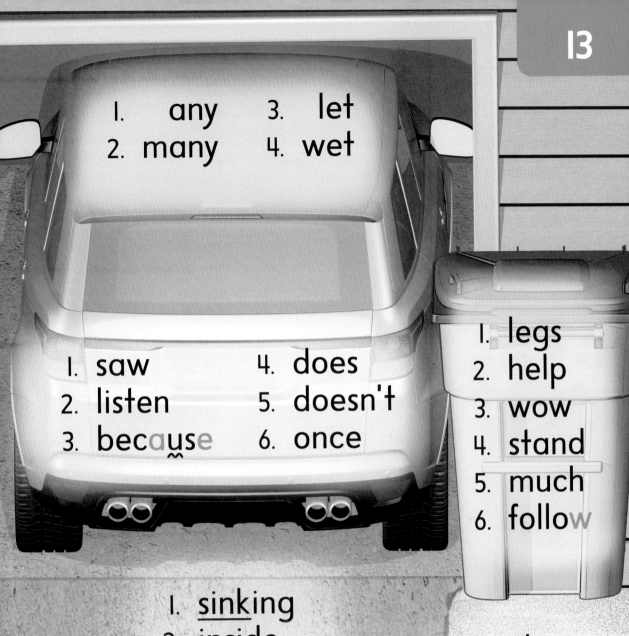

13

1. any
2. many
3. let
4. wet

1. saw
2. listen
3. because
4. does
5. doesn't
6. once

1. legs
2. help
3. wow
4. stand
5. much
6. follow

1. sinking
2. inside
3. harder
4. return
5. getting
6. rolled

1. close
2. clam
3. otter
4. saving
5. silly

Bob and Sid
Part One

One day, Bob and Sid went for a hike. After they hiked for six miles, they came to a cave. Bob said, "Let's go in that cave."

Sid said, "No, there may be mud inside that cave. I hate mud."

Bob said, "Mud can be fun. Let's go inside and see what is there."

So they went inside. It was d<u>ar</u>k. Bob said, "I can't see."

Sid said, "I feel my feet sinking in mud."

"Me t<u>oo</u>," Bob said. "I think my legs are in mud."

Sid said, "It is h<u>a</u>rd to keep going in this mud. Let's go back."

It was r<u>ea</u>lly h<u>a</u>rd, but at last Sid and Bob came from the cave. Bob said, "Wow, that mud on my legs is r<u>ea</u>lly red."

Sid said, "Yes, and we must get cl<u>ea</u>n before that mud gets h<u>a</u>rd."

Bob said, "I think this mud is getting h<u>a</u>rder now."

More next time.

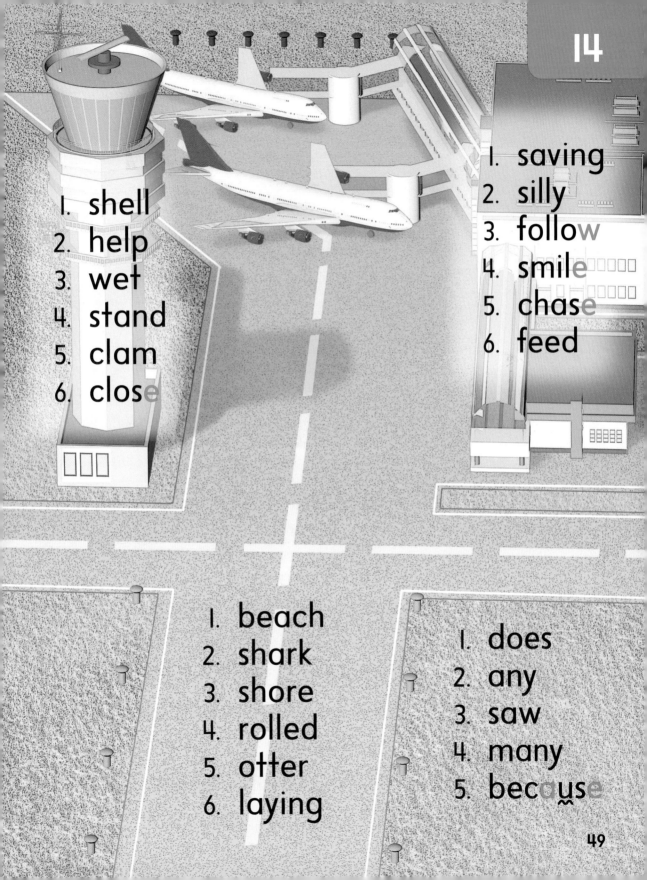

14

1. shell
2. help
3. wet
4. stand
5. clam
6. close

1. saving
2. silly
3. follow
4. smile
5. chase
6. feed

1. beach
2. shark
3. shore
4. rolled
5. otter
6. laying

1. does
2. any
3. saw
4. many
5. because

Bob and Sid
Part Two

Bob had lots of red mud on his pants. Sid did too. The mud was getting hard. The pals had to get rid of that mud.

Sid said, "I see the beach down the hill."

"How will we get down there?" Bob asked.

"Follow me," Sid said.

How did Sid get down the hill? He rolled. And Bob rolled after him.

We can't stand up.

After they rolled down to the shore, they stopped. Sid said, "My pants are so h_ar_d that I can't stand up."

Just then, three s_ea_ls came up to Bob and Sid. One s_ea_l asked, "Why are you laying down like s_ea_ls?"

Sid said, "We can't stand up."

Bob asked the seals, "Can you help us get into the sea?"

A seal said, "Yes. We can roll you in."

So the seals rolled Bob and Sid into the sea.

Then a seal said, "Now that you are wet, let's swim." And they did.

The end.

15

1. weed
2. feed
3. shell
4. bell

1. <u>op</u>e<u>ned</u>
2. <u>swimming</u>
3. <u>happy</u>
4. <u>silly</u>
5. <u>sa</u>ving
6. <u>ot</u>ters

1. clam
2. hunt
3. yelled
4. chase
5. close
6. went

1. front
2. because
3. saw
4. shark
5. followed

A Clam Named Ann

Clams seem to have a big smile, but some clams are not happy. One sad clam was named Ann. Why was she sad? She did not like to stay in the sand with the other clams.

Ann said, "Why can't I swim with the otters?"
Her mom said, "That's silly. Otters eat clams.
They don't swim with clams."

One day, a shark was swimming near the clams. A little otter was swimming near the clams, too. The little otter did not see the shark. As the otter came close to Ann, she opened her shell and yelled, "Shark, shark. Hide, hide."

The little otter hid in the weeds, and the shark went away.

The next day, the otter came back. She said to Ann, "Thank you for saving me. What can I do in return?"

You know what Ann said, and you know what they did.

So if you see an otter swimming with a clam on its tail, you will know who they are.

The end.

16

1. very
2. wet
3. went
4. tell
5. yell
6. where

1. moment
2. front
3. listen
4. because

1. snail
2. feed
3. chased
4. shock
5. Tom
6. beneath

1. we'll
2. I'll
3. I'd
4. shot
5. seemed
6. hunts

1. tap
2. tape
3. hope
4. hop
5. slid
6. slide

Tom and the Shark
Part One

There once was an otter, and his name was Tom.

But Tom didn't listen to his dad or mom.

One day his mom told him, "Don't swim near the caves.

Because there's a shark who hunts in those waves."

But Tom started playing, and he wasn't really
thinking.

He first chased a clam that seemed to be
sinking.

Then he followed two seals that were close to
the shore.

He followed those seals for a mile or more.

At last he stopped to see where he was.

He said, "I saw something swimming the way a shark does."

"Oh, oh," he said, as he hid near a weed.

"I hope this is not where sharks like to feed."

More to come.

17

1. moment
2. very
3. himself
4. someone
5. beneath
6. darted

1. I've
2. he's
3. saw
4. front
5. snail
6. swam

1. such
2. fed
3. there
4. send
5. shock
6. shot

1. anyone
2. trying
3. telling
4. every
5. listened
6. happen

Tom and the Shark
Part One

There once was an otter, and his name was Tom.

But Tom didn't listen to his dad or mom.

One day his mom told him, "Don't swim near the caves.

Because there's a shark who hunts in those waves."

But Tom started playing, and he wasn't really thinking.

He first chased a clam that seemed to be sinking.

Then he followed two seals that were close to the shore.

He followed those seals for a mile or more.

At last he stopped to see where he was.

He said, "I saw something swimming the way a shark does."

"Oh, oh," he said, as he hid near a weed.

"I hope this is not where sharks like to feed."

Tom and the Shark
Part Two

But the shark came closer and showed many teeth.

And just at that moment, someone yelled from beneath.

"For a bigger meal, you can come after me."

The otter who spoke was Tom's mom, you see.

She swam and she dove and bit the shark's tail.

She told that shark, "You're as slow as a snail."

The shark chased Tom's mom as fast as a shot.

And said, "I've got you now." But Tom's mom said, "Not."

Just then Tom got a very bad shock.

His mom just stopped, in front of a rock.

More to come.

18

1. saved
2. smart
3. c<u>ar</u>t
4. street
5. chased
6. drove

1. I'll
2. you're
3. he's
4. shark's
5. men's
6. its

1. which

2. slip

3. such

4. blow

5. rob

6. fix

1. <u>tractor</u>
2. <u>trailer</u>
3. <u>himself</u>
4. <u>herself</u>
5. <u>anyone</u>

Tom and the Shark
Part Three

The shark chased Tom's mom as fast as a shot.

And said, "I've got you now." But Tom's mom said, "Not."

Just then Tom got a very bad shock.

His mom just stopped, in front of a rock.

As the shark came at her, did she stay where she was?

No, she darted to one side, the way an otter does.

The shark hit the rock with such a h<u>a</u>rd blow,

That he said to himself, "Who am I? I don't know."

Then he asked Tom's mom, "Can you tell me who I am?"

She said, "You're a very big seal, and your name is Sam."

So Tom has a pal who thinks he's a seal.

And Sam doesn't know that Tom is a meal.

The end.

19

1. slipp<u>ed</u>
2. men
3. left
4. street
5. sm<u>ar</u>t
6. y<u>ar</u>d

1. Tam
2. send
3. wok<u>e</u>
4. ro<u>w</u>s
5. st<u>ar</u>

1. <u>every</u>
2. <u>happened</u>
3. <u>telling</u>
4. <u>herself</u>
5. <u>we'll</u>

1. saved
2. hear
3. dov<u>e</u>
4. drov<u>e</u>
5. drivi<u>ng</u>
6. times

Will Tam Listen?
Part One

Tam's mom told her, "You can hear well, but you do not listen."

Once, Tam and her mom went up a big hill. Her mom said, "Follow me and st<u>ay</u> on the path." Did Tam st<u>ay</u> on the path? No.

She started to play with the ston<u>e</u>s near the path. Then she slipped and slid down the hill. Ow, that h<u>ur</u>t.

After Tam got home, her mom said, "You have to listen better."

Tam said, "Mom, from now on, I'll listen very well."

But later, Tam and her mom went to the lake. Her mom told Tam, "Do not go swimming in the deep part of the lake."

Tam swam in the deep part of the lake. She did not swim very well. So she started to yell for help. Two men dove in and saved her.

After Tam got home, her mother said, "You have to listen better."

Tam said, "Mom, from now on, I'll listen very well."

More to come.

21

1. c<u>ar</u>t
2. bag
3. left
4. cops
5. sneak
6. drov<u>e</u>

1. <u>some</u>thing
2. <u>an</u>yone
3. <u>an</u>other
4. <u>h</u>erself

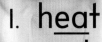

1. h<u>ea</u>t
2. scal<u>e</u>
3. scor<u>e</u>
4. us<u>e</u>d
5. bell
6. fix

1. <u>happens</u>
2. <u>every</u>
3. <u>robber</u>
4. <u>trai</u>ler
5. <u>tractor</u>
6. <u>driving</u>

Will Tam Listen?
Part Two

Tam did not listen to her mom. She kept telling her mom, "I will listen better."

But she still did not listen well. Then something happened that made Tam start to listen better.

Her mom was going to the store. She told Tam, "Do not let anyone in while I am at the store."

After her mom left, a man came by. He said,
"I am here to fix your TV."

Tam was going to let him in, but she said to
herself, "Every time I do not listen to my mom,
something bad happens."

So she told the man, "You will have to come
back another time."

The man went down the street. Tam saw
him trying to sneak into a home. "That man is
a robber," she said to herself. "I must tell the
cops." And she did. The cops came and got the
robber.

Later the cops told Tam, "You were very smart."
And Tam's mom said, "You listen very well."

The end.

22

1. milk
2. woke
3. steer
4. rows
5. store
6. yard

1. Jill
2. fix
3. send
4. bags
5. town
6. field

1. driving
2. loaded
3. tractors
4. trailer
5. waited
6. sleeping

1. apples
2. plant
3. eggs
4. corn
5. things
6. than

Jill Went to Town

Jill lived on a farm that was six miles from town.

Jill told her dad, "It is time to go to the store."

"Well," her dad said, "I need to fix the car. So I can't drive you there now."

Jill said, "I have a plan. I can hike to the store. You can pick me up later."

So Jill hiked to the store. When she got there, she got a cart and filled it. She loaded it with things like corn, apples, eggs, and milk. Then she waited for her dad in front of the store. He didn't show up. She began to think of things that may have made her dad late.

At last she saw her dad. Was he driving the car? No. He was driving a tractor with a trailer.

Jill loaded her bags into the trailer, and her dad drove her home.

The end.

23

1. stars
2. hard
3. farmer
4. started
5. spark
6. yard

1. all
2. fall
3. wall
4. small
5. bang
6. field

1. sleeping
2. ringing
3. thinking
4. flying
5. digging
6. saying

1. bells
2. plant
3. steer
4. miss
5. rag
6. fed
7. lip

The Farmer and the Steer
Part One

There was a steer who lived on part of a farm. One day, the farmer drove his tractor to that part of the farm. The steer was sleeping in the field, and the farmer did not see the steer.

"I will dig rows," the farmer said. "Then I can plant corn in this field."

The tractor dug up one row, two rows, and three rows. When the tractor started to dig the next row, the steer woke up.

The steer said, "What is going on? I see a farmer and a tractor in my field. I don't like tractors or farmers here."

The steer got up and said, "I will send that farmer back to his home."

How will the steer try to stop the farmer?

You will see in the next part of the story.

24

1. f<u>a</u>lse
2. c<u>a</u>ll
3. b<u>a</u>ll
4. <u>a</u>lmost
5. <u>a</u>lso
6. <u>a</u>lways

1. <u>pep</u>per
2. <u>fly</u>ing
3. <u>land</u>ed
4. <u>ring</u>ing
5. <u>throw</u>ing
6. <u>think</u>ing

1. f<u>a</u>ll
2. bang
3. tried
4. stars
5. set
6. base
7. lips

1. chili
2. tongue
3. zero
4. used
5. steer
6. scale

The Farmer and the Steer
Part Two

The farmer was in a field with his tractor. He was digging rows to plant corn in this field. But a steer lived in that field. And that steer was getting set to stop the farmer. The steer went all the way to one side of the field.

Then the steer ran at the tractor just as fast as a steer can run. The steer was thinking, "I will hit that tractor so hard that it will f<u>all</u> over. That farmer will go flying. Then he will leave."

The steer ran into the side of the tractor. There was a big bang. And something went flying. Was it the farmer and the tractor? No. The steer went flying. That steer landed on its back and said, "I hear bells ringing, and I see stars."

The end.

25

1. hiss
2. a_ir
3. rags
4. pen
5. neve_r
6. trie_d
7. sent

1. c_all
2. w_all
3. b_all
4. _always
5. sm_all

1. bas_eball
2. thro_wing
3. mi_ssed
4. _cars
5. _chili
6. sc_or_e

1. _Sandy
2. sp_ark
3. st_arting
4. st_reet_s
5. sn_o_w
6. sme_ll

Sandy
Part One

Sandy did not try to do things. She did not know how to throw a b<u>all</u>, but she did not try.

One day, her mom said, "Let's throw a b<u>all</u> and see if we can hit the w<u>all</u>."

Sandy said, "I do not feel like throwing a b<u>all</u>."

One day, her dad said, "Let's go to the lake and throw stones in it. That is fun."

Sandy said, "I don't feel like throwing stones."

Let's throw snow balls.

Another time, her brother said, "Let's play baseball." Sandy said the same thing she always said.

Then one day late in fall, the snow came down. There was snow all over things. The cars had snow on them. The streets had snow on them.

Sandy's brother was throwing snow balls in the front yard. He asked Sandy to play with him.

Sandy went away from her brother. She said to herself, "I hate snow b<u>a</u>lls, and I will not throw them." Just then, a snow b<u>a</u>ll hit her in the back.

More to come.

26

1. everything
2. saying
3. called
4. flames
5. starting
6. tongue

1. their
2. peppers
3. air
4. wall
5. also
6. rags

1. yard
2. hard
3. fell
4. smell
5. to
6. who

1. spark
2. never
3. tried
4. missed
5. sent
6. pot
7. fed

Sandy
Part Two

Sandy's brother was throwing snow balls in the front yard. He hit Sandy with a snow ball. So Sandy went to the back yard. There, she saw something that was very bad. A spark had landed on some rags. Those rags were starting to burn.

Sandy called to her brother. "Get help," she yelled. "There is a fire next to the wall."

The fire was getting bigger and hotter. The wall was starting to burn.

Sandy said, "I will stop that fire." She made a snow ball and tried to throw it, but she missed the fire.

She made another snow b<u>a</u>ll and hit the fire. "Hissss."

She kept throwing snow b<u>a</u>lls on the fire. At last, the flames stopped.

Sandy's brother came back with their mom. She asked Sandy, "How did you stop that fire?"

Sandy said, "I will show you."

She ran 20 feet away, made a big snow ball, and sent it sailing in the air. It hit her brother.

He said, "Wow, you can throw."

She said, "Yes. Let's do it some more." And they did.

The end.

I'll show you how to throw snow balls.

This is fun.

27

1. s<u>oo</u>n
2. pool
3. moon
4. too
5. food

1. sm<u>all</u>
2. <u>p</u>ots
3. drank
4. both<u>er</u>
5. b<u>ur</u>p
6. fact

1. pen
2. smelled
3. ever
4. never
5. their
6. zero
7. tongue

1. almost
2. peppers
3. drinking
4. called
5. piles
6. everything

Hot Peppers

Some peppers are hot. They do not feel hot if you hold them. But if you bite into them, they burn.

There is a scale that tells how hot peppers are. A bell pepper is not hot at all. The score for bell peppers on that heat scale is zero.

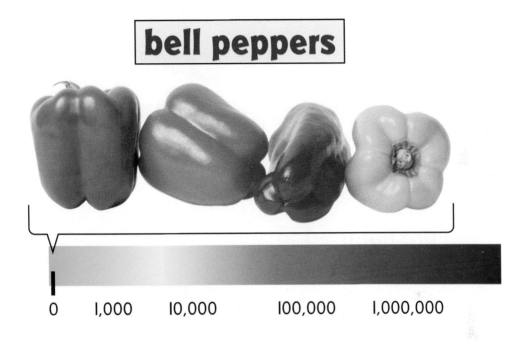

bell peppers

| 0 | 1,000 | 10,000 | 100,000 | 1,000,000 |

Some chili peppers are very hot. Does the burn you feel from eating hot chili peppers go aw<u>ay</u> s<u>oo</u>n? No.

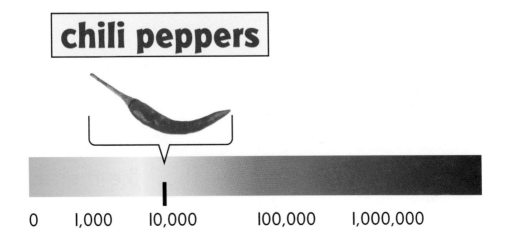

chili peppers

| 0 | 1,000 | 10,000 | 100,000 | 1,000,000 |

Some other peppers are ten times hotter than very hot chili peppers.

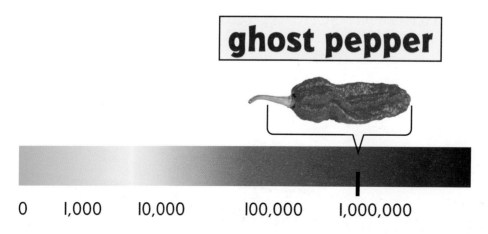

ghost pepper

| 0 | 1,000 | 10,000 | 100,000 | 1,000,000 |

If you are not used to eating hot peppers, and you bite into one of these really hot peppers, your lips and tongue may get sores on them. If you eat one of those peppers, you may also get sick.

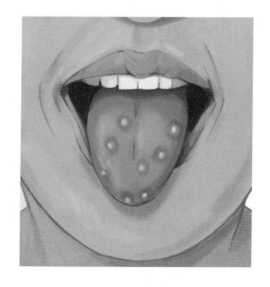

Those who grow up eating hot peppers don't get sores on their lips and tongue. They like the taste of hot peppers.

28

1. chees
2. cream
3. brain
4. heat
5. ha_r
6. colder

1. nonḛ
2. machine
3. knee
4. most
5. anyone

1. s<u>care</u>
2. <u>fact</u>s
3. fem<u>al</u>es
4. <u>swims</u>
5. <u>smelled</u>

1. about
2. collect
3. mammal
4. okay
5. agree
6. between

1. foods
2. room
3. zoo
4. <u>mall</u>
5. s<u>al</u>t
6. <u>al</u>ways

Peppers for Pam's Pigs
Part One

Pam had six pigs. Their names were Pig One, Pig Two, Pig Three, Pig Four, Pig Five, and Pig Six. Pig Six was very small. The other pigs were three times as big as she was.

One day, Pam was going to feed her pigs. She didn't have pig feed for them. All she had were red hot chili peppers. Pam had piles of these chili peppers. She had never fed her pigs peppers, but she said, "I think I can feed my pigs hot peppers. Those pigs eat everything."

So she lo<u>a</u>ded some peppers in a pot and some peppers in a pan. She went to the pig pen with the pot and pan of peppers. She set the chili peppers in a pile and c<u>a</u>lled the pigs. "Here Pig One. Here Pig Two. . . ."

And then the pigs came. The pigs smelled the peppers, but didn't start eating. Pam said, "I don't have any pig feed for you. Why don't you try eating these peppers?"

So the pigs smelled the chili peppers and started to eat.

More next time.

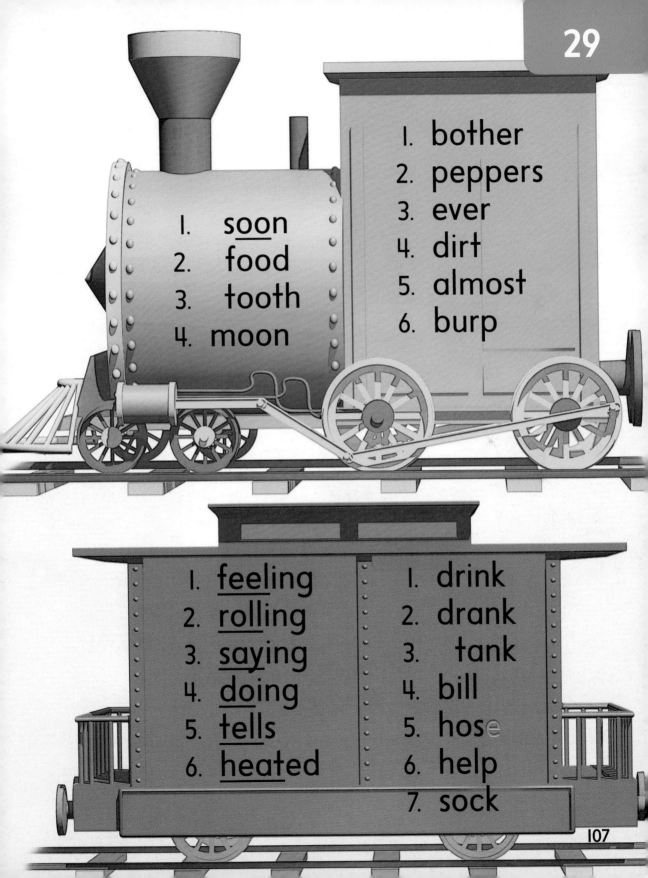

29

1. s<u>oo</u>n
2. f<u>oo</u>d
3. t<u>oo</u>th
4. m<u>oo</u>n

1. bother
2. peppers
3. ever
4. dirt
5. almost
6. burp

1. <u>feel</u>ing
2. <u>roll</u>ing
3. <u>say</u>ing
4. <u>do</u>ing
5. <u>tell</u>s
6. <u>heat</u>ed

1. drink
2. drank
3. tank
4. bill
5. hose
6. help
7. sock

Peppers for Pam's Pigs
Part Two

The pigs were eating Pam's red hot peppers. All at once, Pig Three stopped eating and started to turn red. Then Pig Five turned red. Soon almost all the pigs were red. The red pigs ran to the drinking pan in the pen and began to drink. The pigs drank and drank. Then those pigs ran here and there, eating dirt to get rid of the hot taste.

The only pig that didn't turn red was Pig Six. She ate all the peppers from the pot and all the peppers from the pan. When she was done, she was pink, not red. She smiled at Pam and said, "Burp." That was her way of saying thank you.

Now Pam does not feed peppers to <u>all</u> the pigs.
She feeds peppers to Pig Six. And when Pig Six eats
the last pepper, she <u>al</u>ways tells Pam, "Thank you."

The end.

31

1. comes
2. class
3. feeds
4. darker
5. salt
6. farms

1. cheese
2. drive
3. store
4. hose
5. takes
6. scare

1. none
2. ok<u>ay</u>
3. because
4. machine
5. collect
6. slo<u>w</u>ly

1. <u>t</u>ank
2. <u>m</u>ilked
3. <u>k</u>i<u>ll</u>
4. <u>cr</u>eam
5. <u>b</u>ur<u>n</u>ing
6. <u>f</u>em<u>al</u>e

Jill Went to Town

Jill lived on a farm that was six miles from town. Jill told her dad, "It is time to go to the store because we don't have much food at home."

"Well," her dad said, "I need to fix the car. So I can't drive you there now."

Jill said, "I have a plan. I can hike to the store. You can pick me up there after I get things for us to eat."

So Jill hiked all the way to the store. When she got there, she got a cart and filled it. She loaded it with things like cans of beans, butter, eggs, milk, apples, bell peppers, hot chili peppers, meat, and corn. After she had no more to shop for, she waited in front of the store. Jill waited and waited for her dad but he didn't show up. She began to think of things that may have made her dad late.

At last, Jill saw him. He was not driving the car. He was driving a tractor with a trailer.

Jill loaded all her bags and herself into the trailer, and her dad drove home. The tractor was so slow it was a while before Jill got home.

The end.

32

1. brain
2. ways
3. cream
4. hair
5. cheese
6. main
7. lumps

1. mammal
2. animal
3. about
4. machines
5. picture
6. collect

1. having
2. facts
3. milking
4. whales
5. smarter
6. picked

1. life
2. goes
3. hose
4. class
5. tank
6. kill
7. care

Cows and Milk

Here are some facts that you may not know about cows and milk. Most of the milk we drink comes from cows.

All cows are females. A cow makes milk after she has a baby cow. Cows make more milk than their baby cows need. Farmers collect that milk.

The picture shows a farmer milking the cow. The milk is going into the pail.

Farms that sell milk to stores use machines to get the milk from cows.

The picture shows machines milking cows. Milk goes from a cow into a hose which takes the milk to a big tank.

Before milk is sold to stores, it is heated to kill things in the milk that can make you sick. This must be done with a lot of care.

If the milk gets too hot, it makes lumps and turns into something that is not milk. If the heat is too low, then it doesn't kill the things that make you sick.

Milk and foods made with milk can help take away the burning from hot peppers.

Butter, cream, and cheese are other foods that are made from milk. You can eat or drink these things to help the burn from hot peppers go away.

cream

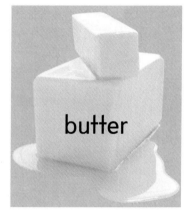
butter

cheese

33

1. main
2. hair
3. salty
4. brains
5. smarter
6. served

1. kinds
2. life
3. ways
4. moles
5. goes
6. tea

1. animals
2. seep
3. mammals
4. pictures
5. sock
6. about

1. classes
2. whales
3. kill
4. facts
5. its
6. having

Mammals

Mammals are a class of animals.

     Mammals are not like other animals in many ways. Here are three main ways mammals are not like other animals:

1. The brains of mammals have parts that make most of them smarter than other animals.

bird
brain

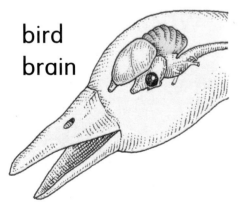

mammal
brain

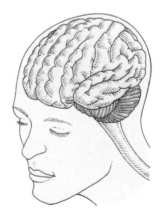

2. After a female mammal has a baby, she makes milk to feed it.

3. At some time in its life, every mammal grows hair.

A cow is a mammal. So a cow has parts of its brain that make it smarter than most other animals. A cow makes milk for its baby. A cow grows hair.

Here are some facts about whales. A whale has parts of its brain that make it very smart. Female whales make milk after having a baby. Every whale grows hair at some time in its life.

So are whales mammals? Yes, whales are mammals!

Pigs, cats, and moles are mammals too.

Does a female pig make milk and feed it to her baby?

Does a mole have parts of its brain that make it smarter?

Do female cats make milk after having a baby?

Does a mole grow hair?

Does a pig have parts of its brain that make it smarter?

Yes, yes, yes to all of these.

You are a mammal. How are you not like animals in other classes?

34

1. m__oo__se
2. t__a__ll
3. f__oo__d
4. __a__lso
5. br__oo__m
6. __a__lways

1. agree
2. between
3. away
4. saving
5. opened
6. soaked

1. burger
2. shark
3. goats
4. parts
5. eats
6. sheep
7. girl

1. out
2. smile
3. meat
4. hide
5. close
6. bean
7. know

A Clam Named Ann

Clams seem to have a big smile, but some clams are not happy. One sad clam was named Ann. She was sad because she did not like to stay in the sand with the other clams.

Ann said, "Why can't I swim with the otters?"

Her mom said, "That's silly. Otters eat clams. They don't swim with clams."

One day, a shark was swimming near the clams. A little otter was swimming near the clams, too. The otter did not see that shark. As the otter came closer, Ann opened her shell and yelled, "Shark, shark. Hide, hide."

The otter hid in weeds. After a while, the shark went away.

The next day, the otter came back. She said to the clam, "Thank you for saving me. What can I do for you in return?"

You know what Ann said, and you know what they did.

So if you ever see an otter swimming with a clam on its tail, you will know who they are.

The end.

35

1. zoo
2. goose
3. moose
4. room
5. broom
6. tool

1. b<u>ea</u>ch
2. f<u>ir</u>st
3. d<u>ar</u>k
4. sm<u>a</u>ll
5. b<u>ur</u>ger
6. r<u>ai</u>l

1. Beth
2. Tim
3. none
4. slowly
5. blowing
6. okay

1. scare
2. hates
3. knees
4. yelling
5. rotten
6. nuts

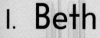

A Swim for Bob
Part One

Bob can swim like a seal. None of his pals can swim well. Tim can not swim at all. Beth can swim, but she hates to swim. And Beth swims very slowly.

One day Bob was with Beth and Tim. Bob said, "Why don't we all go for a swim at the beach? We can have fun in the waves."

Tim said, "Not me. I don't like to go near big waves."

Beth said, "I hate to swim."

"Come on," Bob said. "We will have lots of fun in the waves."

At first, Bob's pals didn't feel like going with him. But after a while, they said, "Okay. We will go with you."

Before Bob went swimming, he had to ask his dad. He asked, "Can you let us take the van to the beach so we can go for a swim in the waves?"

His dad said, "Okay. But you must be home before it gets dark."

"Yes," Bob said. "We will be back by then."

More to come.

36

1. able
2. out
3. <u>why</u>
4. dove
5. fries
6. steak

1. we'll
2. they'll
3. she'll
4. I'll
5. won't
6. aren't

1. knees
2. blowing
3. yelling
4. between
5. agree
6. slower

1. <u>coming</u>
2. <u>calling</u>
3. <u>having</u>
4. <u>standing</u>
5. <u>setting</u>
6. <u>anything</u>

A Swim for Bob
Part Two

Bob and his pals were on the<u>ir</u> way to swim in the waves. Beth drove the van. Tim sat in back. He kept saying, "Why did I agree to go to the beach? Waves scare me."

Beth kept saying, "Yes, why did I agree to go? I hate to swim."

Bob kept saying, "But we will have lots of fun."

When the pals got to the beach, the wind was blowing hard, and the waves were big. Bob dove into the waves and swam like a seal. Tim went in the waves up to his knees and then said, "This is not for me."

Beth went in the waves, but she swam like a
cat. She didn't like it. And she kept yelling to Bob,
"Wait for me. Don't swim so fast."

But Bob didn't hear her. He was going over the
waves, under the waves, and between the waves.

More to come.

---

37

1. week
2. m**all**
3. met
4. grass
5. okay
6. st**e**ak

1. find
2. out
3. able
4. g**ir**l
5. sheep
6. seep

1. <u>driving</u>
2. <u>diving</u>
3. <u>calling</u>
4. <u>coming</u>
5. <u>rotten</u>
6. <u>wasn</u>'t

1. car**e**d
2. scared
3. <u>soon</u>
4. moon
5. nuts
6. huts

Many foods are pasteurized before they are sold.

A Swim for Bob
Part Three

Beth said, "I can't keep up with Bob." So after a while, she came from the waves and sat on the beach. Soon the sun started to go down. Beth began calling to Bob. "Bob, it's time to go home."

But Bob didn't hear her. He was diving and swimming and rolling and having so much fun that he didn't know it was time to leave.

At last, he stopped swimming and came out of the waves on to the beach. "Wasn't that fun?" he asked Beth.

"No," she said. "Now let's get Tim and go home."

But where was Tim? Beth and Bob went up and down the beach, but they didn't see Tim. They went to the van, but they didn't see him there. By now, the sun was down, and Bob was getting scared. He kept thinking, "I hope Tim is okay."

More to come.

38

1. yard
2. week
3. yes
4. ever
5. drop
6. steak

1. setting
2. standing
3. trying
4. until
5. hamburgers
6. somebody

1. find
2. saw
3. girl
4. beans
5. fries
6. meat

1. sky
2. mall
3. sheep
4. zoo
5. room
6. where

A Swim for Bob
Part Four

The sun had set, and the m<u>oo</u>n and stars were in the sky. Bob and Beth were trying to find Tim. They were standing next to the van. All at once, somebody said, "What time is it?"

Bob turned and saw Tim coming out of the van. Tim said, "I was sleeping in the back seat."

"Wow," Bob said. "Am I ever happy to see you."

Beth said, "Yes, I'm happy too. But we are late. Let's go home."

So the three pals got in the van and drove home.

Bob's dad met them as they drove up. Was Bob's dad happy? No.

Later that week, Beth and Tim went for a bike ride to the zoo. Did Bob go with them? No. He had to stay in his room.

Ten days after Bob came home late, Beth and Tim went to the mall. Did Bob go with them? No. He had to stay in his yard.

How many days do you think Bob will have to stay home?

The end.

39

1. apples
2. anything
3. hamburgers
4. rotten
5. until
6. likely

1. meat
2. goats
3. eats
4. parts
5. beans
6. tall

1. likes
2. sheep
3. steak
4. seeds
5. fries
6. steep

1. grass
2. nuts
3. moose
4. plants
5. crack
6. bragged

What Animals Eat

Some animals eat only grass or parts from other plants.

Some animals eat parts from other animals. Meat, like steak and hamburgers, comes from animals.

Some animals eat plants and other animals.

All of us can eat foods made from plants and animals. Some of you m<u>ay</u> not like to eat meat from animals. Those of you who do not eat meat eat things like cheese, nuts, seeds, beans, and other parts of plants.

Some birds eat seeds and nuts of plants.

Some birds eat other animals.

Mammals like cows, goats, m<u>oo</u>se, and sheep don't eat animals. They eat food from plants.

One farm animal eats plants and meat. That animal eats anything you eat. This animal really likes <u>bu</u>rgers and fri<u>e</u>s, apples and corn. This mammal <u>al</u>so likes a lot of things you don't eat. This farm animal likes rotten food that you throw aw<u>ay</u>. That farm animal is a pig.

Pigs can eat almost everything.

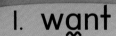

41

1. want
2. else
3. lies
4. pass
5. pack
6. find

1. bragging
2. yelling
3. throwing
4. saying
5. anyone
6. something

1. listen
2. follow
3. happened
4. smart
5. socks
6. tea

1. home
2. stones
3. lake
4. tried
5. sneak
6. steep

Tam Will Listen

Tam did not listen to her mom. Once on a hike, her mom said, "Follow me and stay on the path." Tam started to play with the stones near the path. Then she slipped and slid down the hill. Ow.

Later, her mom told Tam, "Do not go swimming in the deep part of the lake." But Tam swam in the deep part of the lake. She did not swim well, and she had to call for help. Two men dove in and saved her.

But then something happened that made Tam start to listen. Her mom told her, "Do not let anyone in while I am at the store."

After her mom left, a man came by her home. He said, "I am here to fix your TV."

Tam was going to let him in, but she said to herself, "Every time I do not listen to my mom, something bad happens."

So she told the man, "My mother is doing something in her room, so you will have to come back another time."

The man went down the street and tried to sneak into a home. "That man is a robber," Tam said. She called the cops. They came and got the robber.

Later the cops told Tam, "You were very smart to call for help."

And Tam's mom said, "And you listen very well."

The end.

42

1. else
2. m<u>oo</u>se
3. goose
4. live

1. <u>fo</u>rest
2. <u>fa</u>stest
3. <u>kee</u>per
4. <u>swimmer</u>
5. <u>bragging</u>
6. <u>steeper</u>

1. pack
2. meat
3. meet
4. pass
5. lies
6. tire

1. want
2. out
3. find
4. agreed
5. helps
6. lift

1. line
2. rail
3. teas
4. plane
5. wheels

The Bragging Rats

A pack of rats lived on a farm. The<u>ir</u> home was not far from the pond.

There were two rats in the pack who made the other rats mad. These two rats did a lot of bragging and a lot of yelling at each other. They did not agree on which rat was the best at throwing, or which rat was the fastest at eating. These rats told a lot of lies. The other rats called them the bragging rats.

One time, the bragging rats did not agree on which rat was the fastest swimmer. One rat said, "I can swim so fast that I pass up seals and otters."

The other rat said, "I can swim so fast I don't get wet."

As the two rats were bragging, it started to rain. The dirt under the<u>ir</u> feet started to turn to mud. The bragging rats slipped and went into the pond. They were not able to get out. One rat said, "Help. This pond is too deep for me."

The other rats said, "We will help you get out, but you must stop saying how well you swim." The bragging rats agreed. After that, they never bragged about how well they swam. But they bragged about lots of other things.

The end.

43

1. steepest
2. biggest
3. showing
4. we're
5. they're
6. airplanes

1. rested
2. morning
3. fall
4. sitting
5. forest
6. keeper

1. clock
2. noon
3. cobs
4. met
5. meet
6. basket

1. live
2. else
3. want
4. easy
5. float
6. girl

Cows and some turtles are herbivores.

A Home in the Zoo
Part One

A goose and a m<u>oo</u>se were pals. They lived in a f<u>o</u>rest. Every day, they did the same thing. They went to the pond. The m<u>oo</u>se went into the pond and at<u>e</u> weeds while the goose swam. Then they got out of the pond and sat in the grass. S<u>oo</u>n they went back into the pond. At the end of the day, they went home.

One day, the goose said to the m<u>oo</u>se, "I am getting sick of doing the same thing every day. We meet the same moles and the same birds. We go to the same pond. We need to do something else."

The m<u>oo</u>se said, "Why don't we go live in a zoo?"

The goose said, "That is a fine plan. Let's call a zoo and tell them that we plan to live there."

So the goose called the zoo and told the zoo keeper what they were thinking.

The zoo keeper said, "We have no room for another m<u>oo</u>se and another goose."

More to come.

44

1. want
2. wash
3. water

1. we're
2. trust
3. easy
4. noon
5. balloon
6. boom

1. been
2. look
3. shiny
4. order

1. morning
2. anybody
3. nobody
4. floating
5. sailing
6. showing

1. talk
2. vehicle
3. drop
4. seeps
5. crowd

1. tall
2. steeper
3. steepest
4. hills

A Home in the Zoo
Part Two

After the goose called the zoo, the m<u>oo</u>se was very sad.

"I w<u>a</u>nt to go to a zoo," he said. "Why can't we live in a zoo?"

The goose said, "You know, I can go to that zoo. All I need to do is fly there and land in the pond with other birds."

The m<u>oo</u>se said, "Yes, that's easy for you to do. But I can't fly. So how can I get there?"

The m<u>oo</u>se and the goose started to think, and they kept thinking all m<u>or</u>ning. By n<u>oo</u>n they were still thinking. Then the goose saw something in the pond. It was a fl<u>o</u>ating leaf. And on that leaf were two little bugs. They were sailing on that leaf.

The goose said, "Do you see those bugs on that leaf? They are showing us how to get to the zoo."

The moose asked, "Do you mean we are going to float on a leaf?"

"No," the goose said. "We will float there, but not on a leaf."

More to come.

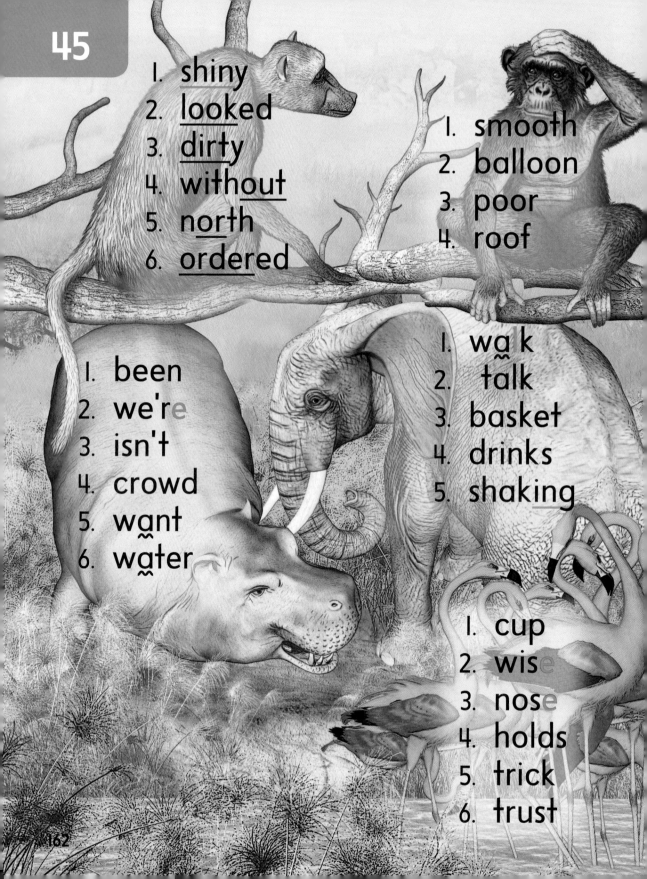

45

1. shiny
2. looked
3. dirty
4. without
5. north
6. ordered

1. smooth
2. balloon
3. poor
4. roof

1. been
2. we're
3. isn't
4. crowd
5. want
6. water

1. walk
2. talk
3. basket
4. drinks
5. shaking

1. cup
2. wise
3. nose
4. holds
5. trick
6. trust

A Home in the Zoo
Part Three

The goose had told the moose that they were going to fl<u>oa</u>t to the zoo. The moose asked, "How can we fl<u>oa</u>t to the zoo?"

The goose said, "We will fl<u>oa</u>t in the sky. We will ride in a big balloon."

The moose l<u>oo</u>ked up in the sky and said, "Oh."

So the goose called a balloon shop and ordered a big balloon. But when the balloon came, the moose started to get cold feet. He said, "I don't know about this. I have never been flying before, and I am scared."

"Oh, come on," the goose said. "Flying is fun. Trust me. You will have fun in the sky."

The moose said, "I think I'm too scared to get in that balloon. What happens if it falls out of the sky?"

The goose said, "Well, I'll just fly away."

"And I'll fall down, like a rock," the moose said. "No thanks. I'll stay here."

More next time.

46

1. folks
2. you'll
3. isn't
4. case
5. fear
6. stair

1. been
2. talking
3. walked
4. wonderful
5. lions

1. apes
2. poor
3. roof
4. smooth
5. baboon
6. tiger

1. taller
2. gathered
3. below
4. shaking
5. wanted
6. looking

1. without
2. nobody
3. floating
4. buses

One kind of carnivore is cats.

A Home in the Zoo
Part Four

The moose was scared. He didn't want to get into the balloon. The goose tried to talk the moose into going. "That balloon isn't going to fall out of the sky," he said. "And I won't go to the zoo without you. The two of us will go, or the two of us will stay here. And I want to go.

The goose did lots and lots of talking that day. By the time the moon was coming up, the moose said, "Okay. I will go."

The next m<u>or</u>ning, the goose jumped into the basket of the balloon. "Let's go," he said to the moose. And the goose kept t<u>a</u>lking as the moose slowly got in the basket. That p<u>oo</u>r moose was shak<u>ing</u> with fear.

I want to be at home.

After the moose was in the basket, the balloon started to go up and up. S<u>oo</u>n it was way up in the sky.

The ride was very sm<u>oo</u>th, but the moose was still scared. He kept saying, "Why am I doing this? I want to go home."

The goose said, "We will s<u>oo</u>n be over the zoo."

More to come.

had   clock   bat

1. On line 1, tell what Jan had.
2. On line 2, tell what Tom had.

47

1. lion
2. baboon
3. tiger
4. ape

1. taller
2. gathered
3. believe
4. morning
5. nearly

1. north
2. doing
3. below
4. inside
5. biggest

1. feather
2. shiny
3. folks
4. drop
5. crowds

1. wonderful
2. forgot
3. everybody
4. staircase

1. took
2. ready
3. long
4. water

A Home in the Zoo
Part Five

It was nearly dark out. The m<u>oo</u>n was big and shiny. The goose said, "I see the zoo below."

The moose said, "I want this ride to be over."

The goose said, "I will try to land the balloon where the other moose live."

But just as the balloon was getting set to land
on the <u>roo</u>f of the moose home, a wind came up.
The balloon went n<u>or</u>th. And when the balloon
landed, the moose l<u>oo</u>ked out and said, "What is
this? We are not in the moose home."

The next morning, lots of folks came to the zoo to see the lions and tigers. They came to see the birds and the apes. But the biggest crowds gathered near the baboon home.

The folks did not believe what they saw. Inside were 56 baboons, one hot air balloon, and one big moose. That moose had three baby baboons and one goose sitting on his back.

Everybody said, "What a wonderful show."

The end.

The   fish   kite

1. On line 1, tell what the goat had.
2. On line 2, tell what the shark had.

48

1. anyone
2. anybody
3. staircases
4. visit
5. yellow
6. forgot

1. feathers
2. took
3. long
4. vehicle
5. listened

1. nose
2. shut
3. lunch
4. trick
5. fool
6. smarter

1. lift
2. planes
3. wheels
4. fear
5. supper
6. rails

Who is Smarter?
Part One

One time the bragging rats yelled and bragged for a week. They were bragging about how smart they were. The rat with the big yellow teeth kept saying, "I am so smart that I know more things than anyone else."

The other bragging rat kept saying, "I forgot more things than you will ever know."

Those bragging rats told many lies. By the end of the week, the other rats were not able to stand it any more. So some of the rat pack went to the wise old rat. They asked him, "What can we do to stop the bragging rats from yelling all the time?"

The wise old rat said, "I think I have a plan that will keep them from talking for many days."

These feathers are part of my plan.

Later that day, the wise old rat went to visit the bragging rats. The wise old rat had two feathers. He told the other rats that these feathers were part of his plan to make the bragging rats stop talking. What did the wise old rat plan to do with the feathers?

You will find out next time.

mail

1. On line 1, tell what the man had.

2. On line 2, tell what the girl had.

49

1. says
2. both
3. ready
4. took
5. feather
6. vehicles

1. something
2. anything
3. anybody
4. everyone
5. forgot
6. airplanes

1. lift
2. stays
3. lead
4. tricks
5. nose
6. fool

1. longer
2. talking
3. smartest
4. listening
5. waved
6. bumps

All of us are omnivores.

Who is Smarter?
Part Two

The wise old rat had a plan to make the bragging rats stop talking and yelling. He took two feathers with him. They were part of his plan.

When he came up to the bragging rats, the rat with yellow teeth was saying, "I am so smart that nobody can fool me or play tricks on me."

The other bragging rat started to say something, but the wise old rat said, "Wait. There is a way to see who is the smartest rat."

A smart rat can . . .

The bragging rats stopped yelling and listened. The wise old rat waved the feathers at the bragging rats and said, "A smart rat can stand so a feather stays on the end of his nose. If you can keep the feather on the end of your nose for a long time, you are very smart."

The rat with the yellow teeth said, "I can keep that feather on my nose for a week."

The rat with the long tail said, "I can do it way longer than that."

More next time.

socks   rocks

1. On line 1, tell what the man had.
2. On line 2, tell what the girl had.

51

1. smarter
2. smartest
3. longer
4. longest
5. smiling
6. running

1. both
2. ready
3. says
4. saw
5. wheel
6. oar

1. lunch
2. sink
3. stays
4. dock
5. trick
6. lifts

1. mister
2. forward
3. winner
4. anybody
5. supper
6. nobody

1. dried
2. bus
3. truck
4. ships
5. boats
6. planes

Who is Smarter?
Part Three

The wise old rat had a plan to keep the bragging rats from talking. He told them that the smarter rat can stand longer with a feather on his nose.

The wise old rat said, "Before you start, let me show you how hard it is to keep the feather from floating away." He set a feather on the end of his nose. Then he said, "You see, it . . ." As soon as he said "you," the feather went sailing into the air.

Then the wise old rat said, "You see, it is not easy to keep the feather on your nose. But if you are very smart, you will think of a way to do it."

The rat with the yellow teeth said, "I know how to do it, but I'm not going to tell anybody else."

The rat with the long tail said, "I know how to do it too, and I can do it better and longer than you can."

"No you can't," the rat with yellow teeth said. "I'm the smartest rat, and I am ready to show you that I am."

This is not the end.

was   tree   pond

1. On line 1, tell what the bird was in.
2. On line 2, tell what the fish was in.

52

1. good
2. stood
3. even
4. says
5. both
6. leader

1. yet
2. still
3. clock
4. lunch
5. supper
6. hop

1. smiling
2. small
3. winner
4. wanted
5. forward
6. mister

1. head
2. where
3. were
4. here
5. their
6. itself

1. wade
2. bank
3. salty
4. stream
5. pies

Who is Smarter?
Part Four

The bragging rats believe that the feathers show how smart they are.

The wise old rat set a clock near the bragging rats. Then he set a feather on the nose of each bragging rat. He said, "The clock will show us how long you can keep the feather on your nose."

Both bragging rats were smiling, but they did not say a thing. They were thinking, "I know that I can't talk or the feather will float away."

The bragging rats did not talk all day long.
The wise old rat let them take time out to eat
lunch and supper. At the end of the day, he told
them, "We do not have a winner. So you are both
very smart."

"No," both bragging rats said. "I am the
smartest."

So they did the same thing the next day and the day after that. While each bragging rat was standing with a feather on his nose, the other rats were happy. They did not have to listen to lies and yelling. Every now and then, a rat walked by the bragging rats and said, "My, my. How smart you both are."

And each bragging rat smiled and said to himself, "Yes, I am so smart that nobody can trick me." Everybody in the rat pack was happy.

The end.

cat	bell	shell

1. On line 1, tell what the cat had.
2. On line 2, tell what the man had.

53

1. <u>q</u>uick
2. queen
3. quit

1. cheer
2. seas
3. raft
4. hops
5. creep
6. trucks

1. walk
2. wants
3. else
4. talked
5. good
6. forward

1. <u>everywhere</u>
2. <u>somebody</u>
3. <u>needed</u>
4. <u>himself</u>
5. <u>funny</u>
6. <u>boating</u>

1. Gorman
2. Joan
3. lead
4. toads
5. dried
6. stream

Gorman and the Toads
Part One

Gorman did not see well. He wanted to go for a boat ride, but he needed somebody to lead him down to the lake. He asked all the other goats, "Who wants to go for a boat ride with me?"

Only one goat said, "I do. I do."

That goat was Joan. Gorman didn't want to go with her because she talked funny. She didn't say things one time. She said them two times. Anybody else says, "It's a fine day for boating."

Joan says, "It's a fine day for boating. It's a fine day for boating."

Joan was the only goat who wanted to go boating with Gorman. So at last Gorman told Joan, "Okay. Let's go."

Joan said, "First, I have to ask my mother. First, I have to ask my mother."

Gorman said to himself, "This will not be a lot of fun. This will not be a lot of fun."

Joan ran home and talked to her mother. Then she came back and told Gorman, "My mother said I can't get wet. My mother said I can't get wet."

Gorman said, "How can you get wet? You will be in a safe boat."

More to come.

under   car   tree

1. On line 1, tell what was under the car.
2. On line 2, tell what was under the star.

54

1. <u>q</u>ueen
2. s<u>q</u>ueak
3. <u>q</u>uick

1. give
2. g<u>oo</u>d
3. stood
4. even
5. how
6. who

1. dock
2. hope
3. blame
4. web
5. yet
6. s<u>oo</u>n

1. <u>leadi</u>ng
2. <u>talki</u>ng
3. <u>aski</u>ng
4. <u>miste</u>r
5. <u>hoppe</u>d
6. <u>holds</u>

1. stream
2. spid<u>er</u>
3. stink
4. stump

201

Gorman and the Toads
Part Two

Joan and Gorman were on their way to the lake. Joan was leading Gorman. She was also talking and talking.

Gorman was thinking, "This may not be a good plan." Gorman and Joan walked and walked. Gorman kept asking, "Are we near the water yet?"

Joan kept saying, "Not yet. Not yet."

Get out of my home.

At last, Gorman and J<u>oa</u>n came to the dock where the boat was. Gorman said, "I will row. You can sit on the back seat."

J<u>oa</u>n said, "Oh, I hope I don't get wet. Oh, I hope I don't get wet."

Gorman said, "How can you get wet? Just sit on the back seat, and you will stay dry."

But just as Gorman was getting set to row the boat, somebody said, "Hold it. This is my home. Get out."

Joan jumped and said, "Who said that? Who said that?"

A big toad hopped from under the seat and said, "I said that. Now get out of my home."

Gorman said, "Who is talking?"

Joan said, "It's a toad. It's a toad."

Gorman said, "Well, Mister Toad, we are going for a boat ride, and you can't stop us."

More next time.

card   moon

1. On line 1, tell what a star is over.

2. On line 2, tell what a lamp is over.

55

1. laugh
2. head
3. lesson
4. stood
5. both

1. before
2. below
3. become
4. believe
5. because
6. between

1. even
2. sink
3. sank
4. drop
5. flies

1. hug
2. oars
3. much
4. hopped
5. filled
6. skin

1. rafts
2. quickly
3. stink
4. taking
5. queens

Gorman and the Toads
Part Three

A toad came out from below the back seat. That toad told Gorman and J<u>oa</u>n that the boat was his home. He said, "Leave now, or you will s<u>oo</u>n be in the w<u>a</u>ter."

Gorman asked, "What do you mean?"

The toad said, "If you do not leave, I will sink this boat."

Gorman said, "Ho, ho. You are much too small to sink a boat."

"I have help," the toad said as he hopped up on the seat. "One call from me, and this boat will be filled with toads. They will sink the boat, and you will be in the water."

I will tell you once more.

Joan said, "Oh, I can't go in the water. Oh, I can't go in the water."

Gorman said, "Don't even listen to that little toad. There is no way he can sink this boat."

The toad hopped to the front of the boat. He stood up on the front seat and said, "I will tell you once more. I am the leader toad. If I call for help, many toads will come. So leave this boat, now."

"No way," Gorman said.

More to come.

truck   balloon

1. On line 1, tell what the ape rides in.

2. On line 2, tell what the lion rides in.

56

1. sank
2. bank
3. slow
4. tow

1. Joan's
2. cheered
3. grabbed
4. running
5. dropping
6. picked

1. hundred
2. head
3. laugh
4. wash
5. oars
6. wade

1. quickly
2. landed
3. lower
4. leapers
5. creepers
6. ones

1. goods
2. balloons
3. roads
4. girls

211

Brothers, sisters, and pals.

Gorman and the Toads
Part Four

The leader toad stood on the front seat and told Gorman and Joan, "I will sink this boat if you do not leave."

Gorman said, "Ho, ho. I don't think we have to listen to what this toad says."

Gorman grabbed the oars and started to row the boat away from the dock. The leader toad quickly jumped up on top of Joan's head and called out, "Brothers, sisters, and pals. Come home."

All at once, many, many toads started to leap into the boat. They jumped from the dock. Some of them hopped from trees. Some of them came flying out of the water and landed in the boat. As more and more toads landed in the boat, the boat sank lower and lower and lower in the water.

Joan called out, "Oh no, I'm going to get wet. Oh no, I'm going to get wet." And she did.

First a little water came over the side of the boat. Then the boat filled up and sank quickly.

More next time.

toad

1. On line 1, tell who will chop.
2. On line 2, tell who will hop.

A smart little girl was in the forest. She did not know where she was. She said, "If I find a stream and follow it down the hill, I will find my way home." That is what the girl did.

1. When the girl was in the forest, did she know where she was? ▮

2. What did the girl look for to follow?

   • a hill   • a stream   • a toad   • a tree

3. Where did the girl follow it?

   • up hill   • a barn   • down hill

   • a store   • home   • a farm

57

1. give
2. again
3. lesson
4. head
5. today
6. hundred

1. leapers
2. creepers
3. slipping
4. dripping
5. sink
6. stink

1. hug
2. roar
3. led
4. bath
5. paint
6. past

1. waded
2. laughed
3. cheered
4. standing
5. taking
6. laughing

1. tow
2. bank
3. black
4. teach
5. blame
6. web

Gorman and the Toads
Part Five

There were almost five hundred toads in the water. There were little toads and big ones, brown ones, green ones, and black ones. Some were fat, and some were thin. Some were leapers, and some were creepers.

The toads were singing and swimming and laughing and having lots of fun. Many of them were yelling, "We did it. We sank that boat."

Thank you . . .

Gorman and Joan were in the water, but the water was not very deep. Joan kept saying, "Oh dear, what will Mother say? Oh dear, what will Mother say?"

The leader toad was standing on top of Joan's head. He was smiling and saying, "Thank you, brothers. Thank you, sisters. And thank you, pals."

A big brown toad smiled and said, "When the leader toad says he will sink a boat, that boat will sink."

Another toad said, "Nobody is better at sinking boats than we are." The other toads cheered and laughed.

At last the leader toad told the other toads to tow the boat back to the bank of the lake. Gorman and Joan waded back and got out of the water. Joan was very wet.

This is not the end.

goat   fox

1. On line 1, tell who will jump.
2. On line 2, tell who will run.

A sn<u>ai</u>l did not like to smile or laugh. One day, she met a bug that was very happy. The bug said, "I can make you smile. I will stick a f<u>ea</u>ther under your shell." The bug did that and made the sn<u>ai</u>l laugh.

1. Who did not smile very much?
2. Who told the sn<u>ai</u>l, "I can make you smile."?
3. What did the bug stick under the sn<u>ai</u>l's shell to make her laugh?

58

1. again
2. today
3. spider
4. slower
5. lesson
6. itself

1. goods
2. could
3. would
4. should

1. live
2. give
3. jump
4. stump
5. game
6. blame

1. dripping
2. ordering
3. teaching
4. biting
5. painting
6. sneezing

1. once
2. place
3. wash
4. laughing

Gorman and the Toads
Part Six

Gorman and Joan were standing on the bank of the lake. The leader toad was <u>or</u>dering some other toads to bring the <u>oars</u> to him. The toads were still singing and laughing. One little toad kept saying, "That was fun. Can we do it some more?"

Gorman and Joan were not having fun. They were dripping wet. Joan was saying, "I hope I dry fast. I hope I dry fast."

Everybody, listen up.

At last the leader toad yelled, "Everybody, listen up." The toads stopped talking and laughing. The leader toad said to the other toads, "Give them their oars, and do it quickly."

Then the leader toad turned to Joan. He said, "Let that teach you a lesson. One toad is small, but many toads can sink boats. Now take your oars and get out of here. Tell your mother Gorman is to blame for getting you wet."

That's what Joan did. She told her mother that Gorman was to blame. She also told everybody else about Gorman and the toads.

Today, the goats still tell the story about the time Joan and Gorman got wet. And the toads still tell the story about how they sank a boat.

The end.

fly	cry

1. On line 1, tell what a girl will do.
2. On line 2, tell what a bug will do.

Two turtles took a trip to the beach. The turtles were sitting in the sun. A man was on the beach looking for stones. He said, "Here are two fine looking stones." And he picked up the turtles and took them home.

1. Who sat in the sun at the beach?
2. Who was picking up stones at the beach?
3. What did that man think the turtles were?
4. Where did the man take the turtles?

59

1. <u>qu</u>iet
2. web
3. sent
4. stump
5. game
6. stuck

1. st<u>oo</u>d
2. sh<u>ou</u>ld
3. w<u>ou</u>ld
4. c<u>ou</u>ld

1. <u>sneez</u>ed
2. <u>paint</u>ed
3. <u>shock</u>ed
4. <u>spid</u>er
5. <u>thank</u>ed
6. <u>creep</u>ing

1. again
2. maybe
3. open
4. bottom
5. <u>ridin</u>g
6. pictures

1. lazy
2. fell
3. snake
4. roar
5. shape
6. load

The Little Bug Bites
Part One

A little bug was the best biting bug, but he didn't bite a lot. His mom told him that good bugs didn't bite if they didn't have to.

One time, he did have to bite. He was playing with Jill, her brother, and her sister. They were on a stump, playing a game of jump.

"I can jump far," Jill said. And she jumped from one side of the stump to the other side.

Jill's brother said, "I can do better than that."
He jumped from one side of the stump and sailed
over the other side. The other bugs cheered. But
when they saw where he landed, they were
shocked. He was in a spider web.

"Help, help," he called. "I'm stuck in this web."

A big spider was not far away, and that spider was starting to come after Jill's brother.

"Help," her brother called again. The spider was creeping closer to Jill's brother. Jill's brother was scared, and so were the other bugs.

Jill said, "What can we do?"

More next time.

drink

1. On line 1, tell what the cat will do.
2. On line 2, tell what the girl will do.

An old farmer had socks that smelled bad.
He said, "I think my socks stink. So I will wash
them in the sink." He did that. Now he says, "My
socks smell good, just like they should."

Now the farmer has socks that smell fine but
a sink that stinks.

1. What smelled bad?
2. Where did the farmer wash them?
3. How do they smell now?
4. What stinks now?

PHOTO CREDITS